The Character & CAREER Connection

by Amy R. Murray, M.Ed.

The Character & CAREER Connection
Grades K-5

$19.95
ISBN #1-931636-45-1

Written by: Amy R. Murray, M.Ed.
Cover Design and Layout by Contract: Ashley S. Linn

Published by: National Center for Youth Issues
                                               P.O. Box 22185
                                               Chattanooga, Tennessee 37422-2185
                                               1-800-477-8277
                                               www.ncyi.org

Printed in the United States of America

Dedication

To my husband,

STEVE,

who is a model for

good character

both at home and work.

The Character & Career Connection published by National Center for Youth Issues, Chattanooga, TN.

3

Acknowledgements

With Special Thanks:

To **NANCY REED** and **ROBERT RABON**

and other staff of National Center for Youth Issues,

my publishers, editors, and supporters.

To my friend **JANET BENDER**

for her encouragement and guidance.

The Character & Career Connection published by National Center for Youth Issues, Chattanooga, TN.

Why You Need This Book

Character is higher than intellect.
—Ralph Waldo Emerson

Having good character means that you are honest and honorable. It also means that you are reliable and responsible. Students who possess good character are trusted by others. They do their best schoolwork and excel academically. These students, upon completing their education, will be much in demand by employers not just because of the skills they have learned, but in large part by the good character they possess.

Some students lie, cheat and steal. These students cannot be trusted. They often are lazy and irresponsible with their schoolwork. Due to their lack of good character, they will have a difficult time obtaining and keeping a job.

Employers are looking for students who not only have high grades in school, but who also possess good character. Businesses are getting more involved in schools because it is understood that the key predictors of an employee's job success and continuance are character traits, not necessarily levels of knowledge. Foremost, businesses are looking for employees who are honest, cooperative, dependable and responsible. (*The Character Education Series*, by Dr. Phillip P. Vincent)

Inez M. Tenenbaum, South Carolina State Superintendent of Education, has stated "Strong character traits, such as honesty, integrity, and responsibility are not only what businesses expect of their employees but also what will lead schools and communities to higher levels of success and achievement."

As educators, it is necessary that we teach character education along with career awareness and exploration. It is crucial that students understand that the development of good character is critical for success in the workplace and in life.

Table of Contents

Introduction

For the past eight years I have continually worked on having a meaningful character education program at my school. Having read Thomas Lickona's *Educating for Character, How Our Schools Can Teach Respect and Responsibility*, as well as many other character education publications, I believe character education training is vital for our students to achieve success.

Two years ago the Palmetto Pavilion Publix store in North Charleston, South Carolina became a business partner with my school, Windsor Hill Elementary. The manager, Tiki Vietri, wanted to support my guidance initiative "Kids With Character." At Windsor Hill, students earn "Kid With Character" slips for demonstrating positive character traits. Every Friday a student is honored as that week's "Kid With Character." Publix provides a special treat each week for the winner, and a large picture of the student is posted in a prominent spot in the Publix store. Teachers and parents agree that this is the most effective guidance program in helping students recognize the importance of developing positive character.

Every year our guidance department sponsors a "Career Day" or "Vehicle Day" in which business partners and parents share their careers with students. It is always important for the students to understand how skills they are learning in school are needed for jobs. In recent years I have noticed business partners and parents talking more than ever about how necessary it is for students to develop positive character in order to obtain and keep a job. No longer is "Career Day" a focus only on the importance of learning school academic skills.

I have come to the conclusion that positive character should be taught as a necessary ingredient for obtaining a career. Students may learn reading, math, and science skills, but just as importantly they must learn to be responsible, respectful, caring, and honest.

My hope is that this book will help all educators, both teachers and counselors, teach students the critical link that exists between good character and a successful career.

Amy R. Murray, M.Ed.

The Character & Career Connection published by National Center for Youth Issues, Chattanooga, TN.

7

Consider These Facts...

- *The Wall Street Journal* says the average business manager spends the equivalent of **1 workday out of 5 (20% of his/her time) just dealing with office politics.**

- A national survey released by the Ethics Officer Association stated that **half of the employees surveyed admitted to acting unethically or illegally** while on the job.

- The Ethics Resource Center, Washington, D.C., found in a 2003 study that nearly one third of respondents say **coworkers condone questionable ethics practices for those who achieve success** using them.

- **Truth telling** is probably the single most cost effective way to make major leaps in productivity and worker satisfaction.

- According to a new University of Michigan Business School study, **small interpersonal acts of compassion** in the workplace have significant, far-reaching effects on co-workers.

- A Gallup study reveals that the best managers are ones who want to see **employees grow and succeed, and who focus on what's best in people.**

- A survey conducted by *The Wall Street Journal International Edition* and the *Nihon Keizai Shimbun* (the leading business newspaper in Japan) showed that **90 percent of the public interviewed considers ethics and values to be "very important"** in building a reputation for good corporate citizenship.

- Showing respect and listening to others increases our own ability to **think creatively, clearly, and effectively.**

Good Character In Action!

If you don't like something change it; if you can't change it, change the way you think about it.

—Mary Engelbreit

Which of these character traits do you possess?
Circle the words that describe you.
Are these traits needed for a good job?

RESPONSIBILITY reliable dependable accountable trustworthy loyal faithful	**RESPECT** look up to follow rules consider feelings of high regard for caring listen to
HONESTY truthful trustworthy honorable upright faithful	**COMPASSION** caring kind thoughtful considerate loving
SELF-DISCIPLINE self-control discipline obedient restraint	**COURAGE** brave strong valiant bold
PERSEVERANCE keep trying never give up determination	**CITIZENSHIP** patriotic help others community-oriented

The Character & Career Connection published by National Center for Youth Issues, Chattanooga, TN.

9

Good Character In Action At Work!

Always be a first-rate version of yourself, instead of a second-rate version of somebody else.

—Judy Garland

How is character needed in the workplace?
Draw a line to connect the character trait to how it is needed.

Honesty	I treat everyone at work with courtesy.
Compassion	Everyone trusts me at work.
Self-discipline	I keep working until the task is finished.
Citizenship	I make sure I get to work on time.
Responsibility	My co-workers know that I care about them.
Perseverance	I am not afraid to try new things.
Respect	I try hard to make good decisions.
Courage	I follow all the rules at work.

The character trait I need to continue to work on is _____.

I can do this by: 1. _____

2. _____

3. _____

The Character & Career Connection published by National Center for Youth Issues, Chattanooga, TN.

Good Character For A Career!

*Attitude is a little thing that
makes a big difference.*

—Winston Churchill

Decide which character trait is most needed for each of the jobs pictured below.
Write your answer in the boxes below.

- **Responsibility**—reliable, dependable, accountable, trustworthy, loyal, faithful

- **Respect**—look up to, follow rules, consider feelings of, high regard for, caring, listen to

- **Honesty**—truthful, trustworthy, honorable, upright, faithful

- **Compassion**—caring, kind, thoughtful, considerate, loving

- **Self-discipline**—self-control, discipline, obedient, restraint

- **Courage**—brave, strong, valiant, bold

- **Perseverance**—keep trying, never give up, determination

- **Citizenship**—patriotic, help others, community-oriented

Responsibility

Being dependable in carrying out obligations and duties. Being accountable for your own actions.

Responsibility

Display the responsibility mini-poster. Read the definition of responsibility to the students. Discuss with the students what it means to be responsible.

Read the book *Horton Hatches the Egg* by Dr. Seuss to the students. Discuss the following questions after reading:

1. Was Horton responsible?

2. What did Horton do?

3. Who was not responsible?

4. What did the bird do?

Explain that Horton made a choice to be responsible. He could have chosen to leave the egg, but he didn't.

What are some choices you make at school every day?

- To finish your work or not

- To walk in the hall or run

- To put supplies away when finished with them or not

- To listen to the teacher or talk when she's talking

Is it important to be responsible at school? Why?

Name some choices students make at school every day. Explain to the students that they should give a **"thumbs up"** if the choice is responsible, and a **"thumbs down"** if the choice is not responsible.

The student who.......

1. always finishes work

2. never puts supplies away

3. talks when the teacher is talking

4. is a good listener

5. walks quietly in the hall

6. keeps a messy desk

7. doesn't complete work on time

8. runs in the hall

9. always tries to do his best

The Character & Career Connection published by National Center for Youth Issues, Chattanooga, TN.

13

Responsibility
Reproducible Bookmarks

 The Character & Career Connection published by National Center for Youth Issues, Chattanooga, TN.

Connecting...
Responsibility & Careers

The best preparation for good work tomorrow is to do good work today.

—Elbert Hubbard

Begin by asking students:

What kind of work do you enjoy?

Is it important to be responsible to get that work done? Why?

Explain that they are going to explore different kinds of work, and find out if being responsible is important. This will also enable students to begin thinking about the kind of work they might like to do as adults.

Reproduce on paper or card stock the cards on pages 16-17. As you read each card ask students to guess what job you are describing. As students guess each job, write it on a chart.

Ask students to name other jobs to add to the chart.

Discuss the following questions:

1. **Do you think these workers have to be responsible? Why?**

2. **Which job is your favorite? Why? What is that worker responsible for?**

Give each student a copy of the *I Will Be Responsible at Work* worksheet on page 18. Discuss with students how they can be responsible at work as an adult.

Responsible
Career Cards

I work in restaurants. Cooking different kinds of food is fun to me. I am responsible for making sure each customer is happy with his food. *Who am I?* (chef)

If you like to travel you'd enjoy my job. I am responsible for many people traveling up through the sky. *Who am I?* (pilot)

I get to live in a park. I am responsible for taking care of our forests and keeping tourists safe. *Who am I?* (forest ranger)

I am responsible for helping keep people safe. Wearing a yellow uniform I jump on a red truck. Horns sound as I hurry to get there, and use the hoses from the truck. *Who am I?* (fire fighter)

I am responsible for making people laugh. I have a painted face. I work in a circus. *Who am I?* (clown)

I work outside in the sun, wind, and rain. I am responsible for using equipment to make houses and buildings. *Who am I?* (construction worker)

I get to work under the sea. I am responsible for studying shells, fish, and seaweed. *Who am I?* (deep sea diver)

I love color and use a brush. Being responsible for changing colors all day keeps me in a rush. *Who am I?* (painter)

Playing sports is my job. Making touchdowns increases my pay. Many times I am responsible for whether or not the team wins. *Who am I?* (football player)

I am responsible for helping people learn about the past. I have fun digging deep in the ground. Sometimes I find old tools, dishes, or jewelry. *Who am I?* (archeologist)

The Character & Career Connection published by National Center for Youth Issues, Chattanooga, TN.

If you like different kinds of cars you'd enjoy my job. I am responsible for repairing cars so they run well. *Who am I?* (automotive mechanic)

If you like children you'd enjoy my job. I am responsible for keeping young children safe and happy. *Who am I?* (daycare worker)

I get to count lots of money. I am responsible for making sure our customers' accounts are correct. *Who am I?* (banker)

Wearing a white coat I stand on my feet most of the day. I work in a store with medicine. I am responsible for making sure people get what the doctor ordered. *Who am I?* (pharmacist)

I plan lessons every day. I am responsible for helping students learn what they need to know. *Who am I?* (teacher)

I work inside and outside. I have fun traveling around in my car. I am responsible for seeing that stores have plenty to sell. *Who am I?* (sales representative)

I get to drive a truck every day. I am responsible for making deliveries on time. *Who am I?* (truck driver)

I love animals even when they are sick. I am responsible for helping them get well. *Who am I?* (veternarian)

Listening to people is my job. I am responsible for helping people when they have problems. *Who am I?* (psychologist or counselor)

If you like computers you'd enjoy my job. I am responsible for fixing computers when they go on the blink. *Who am I?* (computer technician)

I will Be Responsible at Work!

The important thing in life is not your position—it's your disposition.

—Unknown

When I grow up I might like to be a _____.
Here is a picture of me working at that job.

I am being responsible by _____ and _____.

When I grow up I might like to be a _____.
Here is a picture of me working at that job.

I am being responsible by _____ and _____.

The Character & Career Connection published by National Center for Youth Issues, Chattanooga, TN.

Respect

Showing high regard for authority, for other people, for self, and for property.

Respect

Display the respect mini-poster. Read the definition of respect to the students. Discuss with the students what it means to show respect.

Write the word "respect" on a chart tablet. Ask students to brainstorm ways to show respect.

- Good manners
- Helping others
- Kind words
- Smiles
- Listen when people talk
- Share
- Cooperate with others
- Follow rules
- Treat others the way you want to be treated

Reproduce on tag board the "R" cut out on the next page. Give each student an "R" cut out. Demonstrate to the students how to cut the "R" into five pieces. Explain to the students how they will write, or draw a picture, on each piece to represent ways to show respect.

Have students share their respect puzzles and explain why respectfulness is important.

The Character & Career Connection published by National Center for Youth Issues, Chattanooga, TN.

Respect Puzzle

Connecting...
Respect & School

*Do for other people the same things
you want them to do for you.*

—The Golden Rule

Read the students the following story and
discuss the questions on page 23:

Respectful Richard and Rose

Richard and Rose were in Mr. Douglas' fourth grade class. They were hard working students, and they were both also known for being respectful. Mr. Douglas could always count on them to listen carefully during instruction and to follow the school rules. Mr. Douglas also knew that Richard and Rose never had anything but kind words to say. He wished all his students were like Richard and Rose.

One day at school, Richard noticed that John was struggling to open the classroom door upon his return from the media center. John had an armful of books. Richard jumped up and opened the door for John. "Thanks a lot!" John said with a smile. "You're welcome," Richard replied.

Another day, Rose noticed in class that Sally seemed really sad. Sally wasn't playing with anyone at recess either. Rose left her friends to go talk to Sally. "Sally, you seem sad," Rose stated quietly. "My grandma has been sick, and today I keep thinking about her," Sally said with tears in her eye. "I am so sorry, Sally," Rose said with concern. "I remember how sad I felt when my grandpa was ill." Sally brightened a little, "Thanks for talking to me; I already feel a bit better."

When Mr. Douglas called the class to line up to go inside, Richard and Rose accidentally bumped into each other. At the same time, they both said "excuse me" and then laughed!

At lunch Rose told Richard, "You know the last time I bumped into somebody in line, the person called me an ugly name." "I can believe it," Richard said with a nod. "And you know what else?" Richard said, "The other day I was playing with Joey at recess, and he accused me of purposely trying to hit him with the ball." "There sure are a lot of kids who think the worst first!" Rose replied.

After school, Richard and Rose told Mr. Douglas about the mean things they had heard other students say. Mr. Douglas stated that he had noticed also that students were quick to think the worst and often would say something ugly. "You both are so respectful," Mr. Douglas stated with a smile. "I wish all students would follow your example and always use kind words. "Yes, kind words... instead of put downs," Richard said with excitement. "I know what, Richard!" Rose said. "Let's begin a No Put Down Club." "Excellent idea!" Richard and Mr. Douglas said in unison.

The Character & Career Connection published by National Center for Youth Issues, Chattanooga, TN.

Connecting...
Respect & Careers

Ask students:

1. **What does it mean to show respect for others?**

2. **Is it always important to show respect? Why?**

Explain to the students that they will be working in small groups on respect skits. Have the students count off from 1 to 3 around the room. Assign each numbered group a different skit. Group 1 will perform a skit showing respect at home, group 2 respect at school, and group 3 respect at work. Have each group go to a different area in the room to work on their skits.

After each group performs their skit, discuss the following questions.

1. **Why do we want to show respect for others?**

2. **How do people feel when we show respect?**

3. **Is respect important in the workplace? Why?**

Have students draw a picture of respect at school, and then draw a picture of respect in the workplace. You may use the worksheet on the following page.

Discuss the following questions:

1. How were Richard and Rose different from the other students?

2. What happens at school when students don't show respect?

3. What happens when students do show respect?

4. What are put downs?

5. What do you think about the idea of a No Put Down Club?

6. How could your class have a No Put Down Club?

The Character & Career Connection published by National Center for Youth Issues, Chattanooga, TN.

23

Respect Is Needed Everywhere!

Draw a picture showing respect at school. Then draw a picture showing respect at work.
Think about how respect makes people feel no matter where they are!

Respect at School

Respect at Work

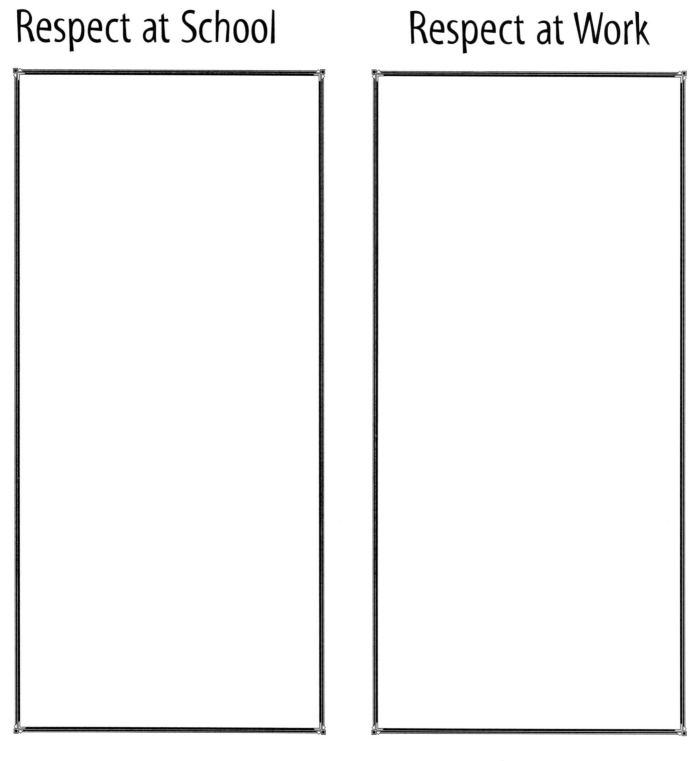

The Character & Career Connection published by National Center for Youth Issues, Chattanooga, TN.

Respect At School

Live good lives... show respect for all people...
try to understand each other.

—Saint Paul

Circle the pictures in which a student is showing respect at school.
Why is it important to show respect at school?

Picking up litter

Talking ugly

Listening

Hitting other students

Tossing trash on the ground

Pushing at school

Showing respect to the teacher

Helping

Sharing

The Character & Career Connection published by National Center for Youth Issues, Chattanooga, TN.

25

Respect At Work

A person is a person because
he recognizes others as persons.

—Desmond Tutu

Circle the pictures in which a business person is showing respect at work.
Why is it important to show respect at work?

Showing respect to boss

Shaking fist at fellow worker

Listening

Hurting property at work

Not listening

Helping at work

Not working

Messy desk

Cooperation at work

The Character & Career Connection published by National Center for Youth Issues, Chattanooga, TN.

Honesty

Having the inner strength to be truthful, trustworthy, and honest in all things.

Honesty

Display the honesty mini-poster. Read the definition of honesty to the students. Discuss with the students what it means to be honest.

Read the students the following story:

Honest Holly and Teresa Thief

Holly and Teresa were both in Mrs. Thompson's third grade class. Holly was honest, but Teresa was a thief.

Everybody knew Mrs. Thompson had the largest and best collection of rocks in the entire school. During Science time students worked in groups to classify the rocks by size, color, and weight. Holly and Teresa were disappointed when Science time was over and the groups had to put the rocks back into the plastic containers.

At recess Holly and Teresa were talking about the rocks. Holly thought the topaz was the loveliest shade of blue she had ever seen. Teresa said she liked the tanzanite best because it was such a dark purple color and tanzanite was becoming very rare. Teresa told Holly that she wanted to take the rocks home. Holly explained that they belonged to Mrs. Thompson, and that perhaps she could ask to borrow them for a night.

That afternoon as Holly was on her way to the bus, she realized she had left her Math homework in the room. Making her way back to the classroom, Holly realized that everyone else was heading towards the buses. Just as she walked into the room, she saw Teresa quickly putting something into her book bag. She couldn't tell what. Holly told Teresa she had forgotten her Math homework sheet. Teresa said that she had also forgotten her Math sheet. Somehow Holly did not think a worksheet was what she saw Teresa put into her book bag.

The next day at school, when it was time for Science, Mrs. Thompson said that one of the containers of rocks was missing. She asked for everyone to search their desks to see if it had accidentally been misplaced. When it could not be found, Holly began wondering if Teresa could have taken the rocks. She knew how much Teresa loved those rocks, and she had seen her mysteriously putting something into her book bag after school. Teresa had even told her at recess that she wanted to take the rocks home.

While all the students were reading silently at their seats, Holly went up to Mrs. Thompson's desk and explained what she had seen after school the day before. Mrs. Thompson questioned Teresa, and called her mother. Her mother found the box of rocks in Teresa's bedroom.

Mrs. Thompson was very proud of Holly for telling her about what happened. Mrs. Thompson told the students that any of them, except for Teresa, could borrow the rocks for a night if they asked her permission. Holly was allowed to take home the rocks that day!

Discuss the following questions after reading:

1. Who was the honest student? Why?

2. Who was the thief?

3. Would you trust Teresa in the future?

4. How could Teresa earn trust again?

5. What advantages are there to being honest?

Connecting...
Honesty & Careers

*Truth is the foundation of all knowledge
and the cement of all societies.*

—Unknown

Discuss what it means to be honest.
Discuss why honesty is important.

Give every student a copy of the Career
Clusters worksheet on page 30. Explain
that honesty is required for all jobs.

Divide the class into groups. Instruct
each group to agree on the job they think
requires the most honesty. Each group should
pick a writer to record their reasons on the
form at the bottom of the worksheet. After
giving the groups about fifteen minutes to
work, have each group choose a reporter to
explain their choice to the class.

The Character & Career Connection published by National Center for Youth Issues, Chattanooga, TN.

29

Honesty In The Workplace

*A lie may take care of the present,
but it has no future.*

—Unknown

Career Clusters

Business & Sales Cluster
Accountant
Bank Teller
Buyer
Cashier
Computer Programmer
Court Reporter
Hospital Administrator
Insurance Agent
Postal Clerk
Real Estate Appraiser
Receptionist
Sales Representative
Stock Clerk
Travel Agent

Personal Service Cluster
Barber
Chef
Child Care Worker
Firefighter
Flight Attendant
Housekeeper
Police Officer
Postal Clerk

Science & Technology Cluster
Aerospace Engineer
Architect
Biologist
Civil Engineer
Computer Engineer
Criminologist
Dentist
Dietician
Mechanical Engineer
Nurse
Physician
Pharmacist
Physical Therapist

Arts Career Cluster
Actor
Artist
Designer
Drafter
Editor
Illustrator
Interpreter
Model
Musician
Photographer
Reporter
Writer

Technical Career Cluster
Aircraft Mechanic
Automobile Mechanic
Brick Mason
Carpenter
Carpet Installer
Construction Worker
Electrician
Farmer
Forest Ranger
Machinist
Pilot
Repairman
Truck Driver
Welder

Education & Social Service Cluster
Counselor
Judge
Lawyer
Librarian
Minister
Psychologist
Social Worker
Special Education Teacher
Teacher

The job that requires the most honesty is:

OUR REASONS ARE:

1. _____

2. _____

3. _____

4. _____

5. _____

The Character & Career Connection published by National Center for Youth Issues, Chattanooga, TN.

An Honest Lawyer & President:
"Honest Abe"

*No man has a good enough
memory to make a successful liar.*

—Abraham Lincoln

Abraham Lincoln is most known as our 16th President of the United States. Abraham Lincoln became President in 1861. Before becoming President of the United States, Abraham Lincoln was a lawyer for twenty years. You may have heard him referred to as "Honest Abe."

While Abraham Lincoln was a lawyer, he gave us hundreds of examples of honesty and decency. Lincoln had grown up very poor, and so he didn't like to charge people much who were poor. Once a man sent him twenty-five dollars, but Lincoln sent back ten of it. He often got his clients to settle out of court to save them lots of money, while he earned nothing. Many times he never charged his clients for his services at all.

An "Honest Abe" Award

Tell the students that you will be looking for students who are honest like Abraham Lincoln, one of the best lawyers and Presidents ever! Duplicate the "Honest Abe" Award notes on page 32 and keep them on your desk for recognizing students when you "catch" them being honest.

The "Honest Abe" Award

This award is given to

_____

for being honest by

_____

Caught being honest by: _____ Date: _____

The "Honest Abe" Award

This award is given to

_____

for being honest by

_____

Caught being honest by: _____ Date: _____

Compassion

Being considerate, courteous, helpful, and understanding of others. Showing care, kindness, friendship, and generosity.

Compassion

Display the compassion mini-poster. Read the definition of compassion to the students from the previous page. Ask students to name ways that they can show compassion.

Read the book *The Giving Tree* by Shel Silverstein to the students. Discuss the following questions after reading:

1. **What did the tree give the boy when he was little?**

   leaves (to make a crown)
   apples (to eat)
   trunk (to climb)
   shade (to sleep in)
   branches (to swing from)

2. **What did the tree give him when he had grown up and was a man?**

   apples (to sell)
   trunk (for a boat)
   branches (for a house)
   stump (to sit and rest on)

3. **How did the tree feel about giving these things?**

4. **Did the tree ask for anything in return?**

Give every student a copy of the "My Giving Tree" sheet on the following page. Have students brainstorm what they can give to others. List their ideas on the board. Ask the students to write their favorite ways of giving on the branches of their trees.

Other ideas:

This makes a great holiday activity! Substitute the "My Giving Tree" sheet that contains the holiday tree. Discuss the many ways people can give to others during the holidays. List ideas on the board and have students write their favorite way of giving on the lines beside the holiday tree on page 36. Students can then decorate their holiday tree!

My Giving Tree

Kindness is never wasted. If it has no effect on the recipient, at least it benefits the bestower.

—Indian proverb

The Character & Career Connection published by National Center for Youth Issues, Chattanooga, TN.

35

My Giving Tree

*Kindness is never wasted. If it has no effect on
the recipient, at least it benefits the bestower.*

—Indian proverb

My favorite way of giving is:

_____

_____

_____

_____

_____

_____

_____

_____

_____

_____

_____

The Character & Career Connection published by National Center for Youth Issues, Chattanooga, TN.

Compassion— Pro or Con?

There is joy in transcending self to serve others.

—Mother Teresa

Write your reasons about why compassion would or would not be needed for the career listed. In the blank box, insert your own career.

Occupational Field	Pro	Con
MEDICINE		
SOCIAL WORK		
CLERGY		
EDUCATOR		
POLICE		
CONSTRUCTION WORK		

Is there a job where compassion is not needed?

_____

_____

_____

The Character & Career Connection published by National Center for Youth Issues, Chattanooga, TN.

37

Careers With Compassion

How many careers that need compassion can you find?

```
F I R E F I G H T E R E D T
L B I K O O E Y F A E N O T
I A E T M I O E M E I O C A
G B H H I A P E T I B C T D
H Y N T N O O A C E S H O T
T S O C I A L W O R K E R E
A I C T S A I C N H L F D I
T T T T T S C O T M I A E T
T T R C E T E U R N B I N C
E E T I R E M N A H R I T S
N R A N A A A S C O A S I O
D S O O O C N E T I R M S R
A P S Y C H O L O G I S T I
N U R S E E N O R N A E Y R
T T T K P R L R L I N T T R
```

babysitter	chef	contractor
counselor	dentist	doctor
fire fighter	flight attendant	librarian
minister	nurse	policeman
psychologist	social worker	teacher

Self-Discipline

The ability to be in control
of your actions so you
can make positive choices.

Self-discipline

Display the self-discipline mini-poster. Read the definition of self-discipline from the previous page to the students. Discuss with the students how they can choose to be self-disciplined.

Read the students the following story:

Lazy Larry and Self-disciplined Sam

Lazy Larry and Self-disciplined Sam were both in Mrs. Montgomery's fifth grade class. Larry and Sam had been in Mrs. James' class together for second and third grade. Both boys were smart and respectful. Both had shown they could be responsible and self-disciplined in second and third grade. Now they were making different choices. Larry was now a lazy student in every way, where as Sam was choosing to be a self-disciplined student.

Sam showed he was self-disciplined by arriving at school on time, listening to the teacher, and completing his work. Sam had to catch the school bus at 7:30 a.m. He made sure his alarm clock was set to go off at 6:30 a.m. every morning so he would be able to get to the bus stop on time. Consequently, Sam was never late to school. Sam showed self-control in class by always listening when Mrs. Montgomery was teaching. He never talked when Mrs. Montgomery was speaking to the students. Sam also showed self-control by completing his class work. Sometimes the work was difficult for Sam and he would have to stop to ask Mrs. Montgomery questions. But, Sam made sure that he always continued to work until the assignment was done.

Larry on the other hand, was a lazy student who was often late to school, talked when the teacher was talking, and seldom completed his work. Larry was also supposed to catch the bus at 7:30 a.m. Larry stayed up late some school nights, and then would not get out of bed on time the next morning. Often Larry missed the bus and was late to school. Some days he would even tell his mother that he didn't feel well so that he could stay home. Larry did have lots of friends in Mrs. Montgomery's class, so he couldn't keep himself from talking to the students who sat near him. He often got in trouble for talking while the teacher was talking. When there was an assignment to complete Larry often did not want to do it. He thought it was silly to have to write down something if he understood it in his head.

Mrs. Montgomery was often frustrated by Lazy Larry. Most of her students were self-disciplined and tried to listen and do their work well. One day Mrs. Montgomery could not help saying to Lazy Larry, "Larry, if you are ever going to amount to anything you must try to be self-disciplined!"

Discuss the following questions after reading the story:

1. **What character trait does Sam have that Larry needs?**

2. **Which student is successful in school?**

3. **How does a student show that he/she is self-disciplined?**

4. **Can Larry change his behavior choices? How?**

5. **Why do students need to be self-disciplined?**

Connecting...
Self-discipline & Careers

Explain that one way to show self-discipline is by getting to school on time.

Ask students:
Is it important to get to school on time? Why?

Do workers need to get to their jobs on time? Why?

Give students a copy of the worksheet on the next page.

After students have completed the worksheet discuss these questions:

1. **What is your job?**

2. **What time does school begin?**

3. **What happens when you don't get to school on time?**

4. **What job would you like to have when you grow up?**

5. **Will you need to get to work on time? Why?**

The Character & Career Connection published by National Center for Youth Issues, Chattanooga, TN.

41

What Time Will You Go To Work?

Do what you can, with what you have, where you are.

—Theodore Roosevelt

Draw the hands on the clock to show what time these people go to work.
Do they need to get to work on time?

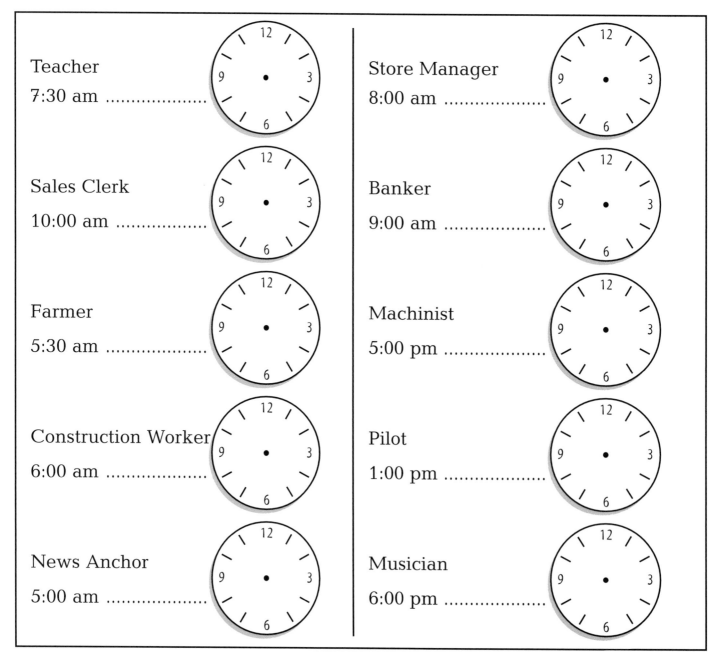

Teacher

7:30 am ....

Sales Clerk

10:00 am ....

Farmer

5:30 am ....

Construction Worker

6:00 am ....

News Anchor

5:00 am ....

Store Manager

8:00 am ....

Banker

9:00 am ....

Machinist

5:00 pm ....

Pilot

1:00 pm ....

Musician

6:00 pm ....

The Character & Career Connection published by National Center for Youth Issues, Chattanooga, TN.

How Well Do You Listen?

He that can quietly endure overcomes.

—English proverb

It takes self-discipline to be a good listener. To be successful at work, you must be able to listen to what a boss or co-worker tells you.

Practice listening to a friend. Ask a friend to tell you about his favorite subject in school. Be sure to look at your friend and pay close attention to what he/she tells you.

Write what your friend said here:

_____

_____

_____

_____

Now ask your friend if you understood correctly!

Try to listen even better this time! Ask your friend to tell you about something funny that happened to him. Be sure to look at your friend and pay close attention to what he/she tells you.

Write what your friend said here:

_____

_____

_____

Now ask your friend if you understood correctly!

Is it important for workers to listen? Why?

_____

_____

The Character & Career Connection published by National Center for Youth Issues, Chattanooga, TN.

43

What Goals Do You Want To Achieve?

The person who properly disciplines himself to do those things that he does not especially care to do, becomes successful.

—Frank Leahy

It takes self-discipline to achieve goals at both school and work.
Here is an example of how to set a goal.

1. Set a reachable goal: *"I want to learn to read better."*

2. Write out steps for reaching that goal: *"I will read 3 books every week."*

3. Stay self-disciplined until you reach that goal: *"I will keep reading even when there are other things I'd rather do."*

4. Evaluate your progress: *"My reading is getting better with every book I read."*

Now write your own school-related goal.

1. My goal: _____

2. My steps for reaching the goal: _____

_____

_____

3. Am I staying self-disciplined? _____

4. How is my progress toward the goal? _____

Now write your own career related goal.

1. My career goal: _____

2. My steps for reaching the goal: _____

_____

_____

3. Am I staying self-disciplined? _____

4. How is my progress toward the goal? _____

Courage

Being brave in difficult times, meeting danger without fear; daring.

Courage

Display the courage mini-poster. Read the definition of courage to the students. Discuss with the students why it is necessary to have courage.

Read the book *Harriet and the Roller Coaster* by Nancy Carlson to the students. Discuss the following questions after reading:

1. **What did George tell Harriet about the roller coaster?**

2. **How did Harriet feel?**

3. **What did Harriet decide to do?**

4. **When do you feel scared?**

5. **What can you do about your fears?**

Give the students a copy of the acrostic worksheet for courage on the following page. Explain to the students that they will write a word or phrase from each letter in the word "courage" that explains the word's meaning. After giving the students 10-15 minutes to complete the acrostic worksheet, have them share their answers.

 The Character & Career Connection published by National Center for Youth Issues, Chattanooga, TN.

What Does Courage Mean To You?

We become brave by doing brave acts.

—Aristotle

Look at each letter in the word courage.
Write a word or phrase beginning with each letter
in the word "courage" that explains what courage means.

The Character & Career Connection published by National Center for Youth Issues, Chattanooga, TN.

47

Courageous Careers

How many courageous careers can you find?

```
R  A  I  A  G  N  H  I  I  Y  C  E  T  E  F  E  G
E  T  A  E  U  P  T  O  N  M  H  F  A  H  Y  I  U
K  A  S  U  H  I  F  P  R  F  R  L  T  E  T  C  F
R  E  U  G  I  T  U  M  I  S  S  I  O  N  A  R  Y
O  N  F  O  R  E  S  T  R  A  N  G  E  R  F  P  M
W  A  I  N  T  S  T  R  M  E  C  H  A  N  I  C  S
N  I  R  N  U  C  U  E  R  U  A  T  S  L  R  N  U
O  C  E  E  A  E  R  A  S  S  A  O  L  U  N  R
I  I  F  O  N  L  S  T  G  C  R  T  P  R  R  E  C
T  S  I  G  O  L  O  I  S  E  H  T  S  E  N  A  P
C  Y  G  C  R  E  C  I  F  F  O  E  C  I  L  O  P
U  H  H  I  T  E  O  O  C  T  E  N  R  E  R  D  E
R  P  T  N  S  T  O  E  O  Y  I  D  L  S  S  W  N
T  I  E  K  A  R  G  F  C  A  I  A  E  R  N  N  S
S  C  R  O  R  G  R  N  I  U  A  N  F  C  R  F  I
N  E  C  E  C  O  O  N  T  S  O  T  T  E  S  O  R
O  I  L  S  A  F  C  R  R  L  R  R  R  S  L  W  F
C  O  C  L  R  P  A  F  N  T  T  N  C  R  E  S  C
```

astronaut	physician	teacher
missionary	anesthesiologist	construction worker
roofer	pilot	nurse
flight attendant	fire fighter	police officer
mechanic	forest ranger	surgeon

The Character & Career Connection published by National Center for Youth Issues, Chattanooga, TN.

Connecting...
The Wizard of Oz and Courage

Ask the students if they have seen the movie The Wizard of Oz. Explain that The Wizard of Oz has an important lesson on how to be your best to have a successful career. Discuss the movie with the students by asking the following questions:

- **Where did Dorothy live?** *(Kansas)*

- **What was the name of Dorothy's dog?** *(Toto)*

- **What did Dorothy's house land on?** *(the wicked witch)*

- **How did Dorothy get to Oz?** *(by following the yellow brick road)*

- **Who were the three friends Dorothy met on the way to Oz?** *(the scarecrow, the tin man, the cowardly lion)*

- **What did the scarecrow want to get from the wizard?** *(a brain)*

- **What did the tin man want?** *(a heart)*

- **What did the cowardly lion want?** *(courage)*

- **Did they get what they wanted from the wizard?** *(No, they had what they wanted all along.)*

- **How did the scarecrow show he had a brain?** *(He invented a plan for rescuing Dorothy.)*

- **How did the tin man show he had a heart?** *(He cried when Dorothy was captured by the witch.)*

- **How did the cowardly lion show he had courage?** *(He went into the castle to rescue Dorothy from the witch.)*

- **Do you have a brain, a heart, and courage?** *(Absolutely!)*

Give the students a copy of the handout on the next page. Discuss with the students how use of their brain, heart, and courage will help them be more successful at school and with a career.

To do your best in school so you
can have a good career you need:

A brain...
to think!

A
heart...
to care about
learning!

And courage...
to ask questions and try what is hard!

To do your best in school so you
can have a good career you need:

A brain...
to think!

A
heart...
to care about
learning!

And courage...
to ask questions and try what is hard!

Perseverance

To persevere means to stick to a purpose or an aim; never giving up what one has set out to do.

Perseverance

Display the perseverance mini-poster. Read the definition of perseverance to the students. Discuss with the students why it is necessary to have perseverance.

Read Aesop's Fable, *The Tortoise and the Hare.*

The Tortoise and the Hare

A hare made fun of a tortoise. "How slow you are!" he said. "You just creep along!"

"Do I?" said the tortoise. "Try a race with me and I'll beat you."

"Ha-ha, you can't beat me," said the hare. "I will race you and beat you! Who can stand at the finish line to make sure the race is fair?"

"Let's ask the fox," said the tortoise.

The fox showed them where to begin the race and where to finish. The fox waited at the finish line.

The race began, and the tortoise lost no time. He started out at once and continued slowly.

The hare ran along quickly for awhile until he had left the tortoise far behind. He knew he could reach the finish line quickly, so he lay down under a tree and took a nap.

The hare woke up and remembered the race. He jumped up and ran as fast as he could. But when he reached the finish line the tortoise was already there!

"Slow and steady wins the race," said the fox.

Discuss the following questions:

1. **Who did you think would win the race? Why?**

2. **How was the tortoise able to beat the hare?**

3. **What does this story teach us about perseverance?**

Connecting...
Perseverance & Careers

Read the book *The Little Engine That Could* by W. Piper to the students. Discuss the following questions after reading:

1. **Who had perseverance in the story?**

2. **How was the little blue engine able to do the job?**

3. **Why couldn't the other engines help?**

4. **Who did not have perseverance?**

5. **How can you achieve what you want?**

6. **Can you have any job you wish to?**

Give the students a copy of the worksheet on the following page. Instruct students to think about a hard goal they want to achieve. After students complete the sentence they may color the picture of the little blue engine.

The Character & Career Connection published by National Center for Youth Issues, Chattanooga, TN.

53

The Little Blue Engine Could, And You Can, Too!

I can _____.

The Character & Career Connection published by National Center for Youth Issues, Chattanooga, TN.

Connecting...
Perseverance & Careers

Read the book *Amazing Grace* by Mary Hoffman to the students. Discuss the following questions after reading:

1. **Did Grace have perseverance?**

2. **How do we know she had perseverance?**

3. **Do you believe that you can be anything you want to be?**

4. **How can you become who you want to be?**

Have students brainstorm things that are hard for them to learn to do. List their ideas on the board or a chart. Explain to the students they can learn to do these things as long as they keep on trying and never give up. We must have perseverance to learn to do difficult things.

Duplicate the following page as stickers for the students. You can make this design using *Print Shop Deluxe*, and then run sheets of labels through your printer. Or you could duplicate the page on crack and peel.

The Character & Career Connection published by National Center for Youth Issues, Chattanooga, TN.

55

Reproducible Stickers
for Perseverance

The Character & Career Connection published by National Center for Youth Issues, Chattanooga, TN.

Perseverance— Yes or No?

No one ever became a success all at once.

—Unknown

Read each of the behaviors listed below.
If the behavior is one which demonstrates perseverance write "yes."
If it does not show perseverance write "no."

_____ 1. head down on desk during teacher instruction

_____ 2. completing hard work

_____ 3. listening to teacher instruction when tired

_____ 4. deciding not to attend school after alarm
clock doesn't sound

_____ 5. finishing a lengthy school project

_____ 6. staying late at work to finish some tasks

_____ 7. leaving work early every Friday

_____ 8. not completing a work project on time

_____ 9. not listening carefully to directions from the boss

_____ 10. following directions given by the boss and co-workers

When is perseverance needed?

_____

_____

_____

On The Job
With Perseverance

The difference between the impossible and the possible lies in a man's determination.

—Tommy Lasorda

Perseverance means to keep trying; to never give up!

Some workers who show perseverance at my school are:

_____   _____

_____   _____

_____   _____

Some workers who show perseverance in my community are:

_____   _____

_____   _____

_____   _____

I show perseverance when I......

_____ and _____.

I need to work on perseverance by

_____ and _____.

My career goal is _____.

The Character & Career Connection published by National Center for Youth Issues, Chattanooga, TN.

Citizenship

Learning the importance
of contributing to
school and community.

Citizenship

Display the citizenship mini-poster. Read the definition of citizenship to the students. Discuss with the students why it is necessary to have good citizenship.

Have students practice showing citizenship by role playing the following situations that could occur at school:

1. **It is time for the Pledge of Allegiance. You see that Mary is refusing to place her hand over her heart. What can you do?** *(show allegiance by placing your hand over your own heart)*

2. **Johnny is returning to the classroom after having gone to the media center for books. He has such a large stack of books that he cannot open the door. What can you do?** *(open the door for Johnny)*

3. **Outside at recess you and your friends notice lots of paper blown on the ground. You are wondering if a teacher lost some papers she was grading. What can you and your friends do?** *(pick up the papers and give them to your teacher)*

4. **You are in the hallway going to lunch when you see several students running into the cafeteria. You know you are late leaving the bathroom and getting to lunch. What should you do?** *(continue to walk to lunch as it is against the rules to run)*

5. **During Science group work, a friend does not understand how to classify rocks. What can you do?** *(explain to your friend how to classify)*

After completing the role play, have students draw their favorite example of how to show citizenship at school.

The Character & Career Connection published by National Center for Youth Issues, Chattanooga, TN.

Connecting...
Citizenship & Careers

Read the students the following story:

Citizen Charley

Charley was not the smartest boy in the third grade, but he was the best citizen. Lots of Charley's friends usually made A's on tests; Charley usually got C's on tests. He could read okay, but he read slower than lots of the other kids in his class. Charley had trouble learning multiplication. He enjoyed writing stories, and was a pretty good speller.

Since Charley was a good speller, the teacher let him help students who had trouble with spelling. Every Thursday after recess his teacher, Mrs. Brown, let him help students practice their spelling words. Any student who felt unprepared for Friday's spelling test, could sign-up for Charley's help. Charley helped students learn the spelling words by calling the words out and listening to his friends try to spell the words out loud. Charley was patient when his friends had trouble spelling. He simply asked them to write the missed words five times, and then he would call them out again.

One day during recess, Charley saw some paper on the ground so he picked it up. Two days later at recess, Charley found an empty can which he picked up. Charley decided to pick up litter every Monday during recess. Every Monday Mrs. Brown gave Charley a large plastic bag for the litter he would find outside.

Charley noticed as the school year went on that the students in his class were having more conflicts. Usually the conflict occurred because one of his friends was not talking or listening to the other. Charley taught his classmates about giving "I-messages" to explain their feelings to others. He also reminded them to listen when another friend was talking.

Charley became a very popular student because he truly cared about his classmates and his school. He may not have had the top grades, but Charley was smarter than anyone about knowing how to be a good citizen. That is why his classmates called him "Citizen Charley."

Discuss the following questions after telling the story:

1. **What character trait does Charley have?**

2. **How did Charley show that he was a good citizen?**

3. **Would you want to be like Charley? Why or why not?**

4. **What kind of job do you think Charley might like in the future? Why?**

School Rules &
Work Rules For Citizens

Learn to obey before you command.

—Solon

My school rules are:

1. _____

2. _____

3. _____

4. _____

When I grow up, I would like to be a _____.
The work rules I might have are:

1. _____

2. _____

3. _____

4. _____

Is it important to follow rules at school and at work? Why?

_____

_____

_____

The Character & Career Connection published by National Center for Youth Issues, Chattanooga, TN.

Being A Good Citizen At School & Work By Helping

How wonderful it is that nobody need wait a single moment before starting to improve the world.

—Anne Frank

I can help at school by:

1._____

2._____

3._____

4._____

When I grow up, I would like to be a _____.
I will be able to help at work by:

1._____

2._____

3._____

4._____

It is fun to be a good citizen by helping others because

_____

_____

_____

Words To Live By
At School & Work

Character is higher than intellect.
—Ralph Waldo Emerson

If you don't like something change it; if you can't change it, change the way you think about it.
—Mary Engelbreit

Always be a first-rate version of yourself, instead of a second-rate version of somebody else.
—Judy Garland

Attitude is a little thing that makes a big difference.
—Winston Churchill

The best preparation for good work tomorrow is to do good work today.
—Elbert Hubbard

The Character & Career Connection published by National Center for Youth Issues, Chattanooga, TN.

*The important thing in life is not
your position—it's your disposition.*

—Unknown

*Do for other people the same things
you want them to do for you.*

—The Golden Rule

*Live good lives... show respect for all people...
try to understand each other.*

—Saint Paul

*A person is a person because
he recognizes others as persons.*

—Desmond Tutu

*Truth is the foundation of all knowledge
and the cement of all societies.*

—Unknown

*A lie may take care of the present,
but it has no future.*

—Unknown

*No man has a good enough
memory to make a successful liar.*
—Abraham Lincoln

*Kindness is never wasted. If it has no effect on
the recipient, at least it benefits the bestower.*
—Indian proverb

There is joy in transcending self to serve others.
—Mother Teresa

*Do what you can, with what
you have, where you are.*
—Theodore Roosevelt

He that can quietly endure overcomes.
—English proverb

The Character & Career Connection published by National Center for Youth Issues, Chattanooga, TN.

The person who properly disciplines himself to do those things that he does not especially care to do, becomes successful.
—Frank Leahy

We become brave by doing brave acts.
—Aristotle

No one ever became a success all at once.
—Unknown

The difference between the impossible and the possible lies in a man's determination.
—Tommy Lasorda

Learn to obey before you command.
—Solon

How wonderful it is that nobody need wait a single moment before starting to improve the world.
—Anne Frank

The Character & Career Connection published by National Center for Youth Issues, Chattanooga, TN.

67

Teaching Responsibility
Tips for Parents

Being dependable in carrying out obligations and duties. Showing reliability and consistency in words and conduct. Being accountable for your own actions.

What children need to know about responsibility:

Everyone has responsibilities and it is very important children learn that they are expected to accept responsibility for their choices and actions. We can give children small tasks to do, encourage them to finish what they begin, and then show genuine appreciation for what they accomplish. Children must learn to finish any job or duty to the best of their ability.

To help children accept responsibility:

1. Never do for children what they can do for themselves.

2. Encourage children to attempt to do things for themselves.

3. Reward children for their effort as well as for accomplishments.

4. Assign daily chores.

5. Expect children to finish the tasks they begin.

6. Let your children make decisions for themselves.

7. Communicate to your children that you have confidence in their abilities.

The career connection:

Children who learn to be responsible for their choices and actions from an early age develop more confidence and have increased self-esteem. These children accept their mistakes and learn from them. They always try to do their best and are more successful in school. Employers seek out those who are dependable, reliable, and keep their commitments.

Teaching Respect
Tips for Parents

Showing high regard for authority, for other people, for self, for property, and for country. Understanding that all people have value as human beings.

What children need to know about respect:

Children need to learn that everyone has value and deserves to be respected, even those whom we dislike. Throughout life, whether at school, at work, or play, we form relationships with other people. When we treat others as we want to be treated, we develop friends and good work relationships.

To help children become respectful, model and encourage them to:

1. Speak politely and kindly to all people.

2. Show common courtesy by saying "excuse me" and "thank you."

3. Apologize, even when not in the wrong.

4. Be a good listener when others are talking.

5. Be open to new opinions and ideas.

6. Help other people (opening doors, picking up, completing household chores)

The career connection:

Children who learn to be respectful and to value others get along well with others. They have more friends and are included in more social activities. These children will continue to be able to form positive relationships with others as they grow older. Regardless of their career choice, they will be able to listen and share ideas, and have a positive working relationship with others. It is essential that respect be present between co-workers.

The Character & Career Connection published by National Center for Youth Issues, Chattanooga, TN.

69

Teaching Honesty
Tips for Parents

Having the inner strength to be truthful, trustworthy, and honest in all things. Acting justly and honorably.

What children need to know about honesty:

Everyone needs to be truthful to gain the trust of others. Honesty is the key to improved relationships and developing self awareness.

To help children develop honesty:

1. Model honesty by making sure you always tell the truth.

2. Discuss with your child the positive effects of honesty.

3. Praise your children when they tell the truth, especially when they may have felt uncomfortable doing so.

4. If your child tells a lie, state you are disappointed in his/her choice to lie. Be sure to keep the child's self-respect intact.

5. Children sometimes lie to get what they want if they feel their lives are too controlled. If you think this is the case, look for ways to say yes more often.

The career connection:

When honesty and trust exist in a relationship, cooperation is greatly enhanced. For any business or industry to be successful there must be cooperation and trust among the employees.

The Character & Career Connection published by National Center for Youth Issues, Chattanooga, TN.

Teaching Compassion
Tips for Parents

Being considerate, courteous, helpful, and understanding of others. Showing care, kindness, friendship, and generosity. Treating others as you would like to be treated.

What children need to know about compassion:

Being kind to all people at all times is one of the best ways to feel good about yourself and develop a sense of self-worth.

To help children develop compassion:

1. Model showing care, concern, and understanding for others.

2. Encourage your children to make cards to send to others.

3. Together with your child, help someone in need.

4. Encourage your child to develop friendships.

The career connection:

Experiencing compassion at work generates positive feelings among employees and creates positive long term attitudes and behaviors. Whether people experience compassion at work on the giving end or the receiving end, or simply observe it, these positive interactions promote a healthy work environment and increase worker productivity.

Teaching Self-discipline
Tips for Parents

The ability to be in control of your actions so you can make positive choices.

What children need to know about self-discipline:

Children must learn from an early age that they control their actions. They learn that when they make a poor choice, undesirable consequences happen. When good choices are made, there is a positive result. All people must be in control of their actions in order to make positive choices. The ability to set positive goals and work toward them is necessary to achieve success.

To help children develop self-discipline:

1. Discuss ways of showing self-control.

   • Take deep breaths or count to ten

   • Remind yourself of why you should not do it

   • Remember the consequences

   • Remember that you feel better about yourself when you make good choices

2. Set rules and enforce them.

3. Praise children's behavior when rules are followed.

4. Help children set goals and follow them.

5. Teach cooperation skills.

6. Make sure you model self-discipline.

The career connection:

Self-discipline sometimes involves postponing immediate pleasure to reach future goals. Demands for concentration, sustained effort, and sacrifice of leisure time are central in the work environment. Self- motivation and self-discipline are necessary to be successful in a career.

Teaching Courage
Tips for Parents

Being brave in difficult times; meeting danger without fear; daring.

What children need to know about courage:

Everyone has disappointments and obstacles they have to face. We all need courage to conquer our fears and to try new and different things.

To help children develop courage:

1. Encourage children to try new things.

2. Teach them that mistakes are okay, and can be learning opportunities.

3. Help your children face their fears by practicing what is difficult for them (Ex. meeting a new friend for the first time, giving a presentation in front of the class).

The career connection:

Some of the most successful people have been those who faced adversity: Abraham Lincoln was raised in poverty, Beethoven was born deaf, Einstein was considered retarded, and Martin Luther King faced racial discrimination. All of these people gained success despite the obstacles they faced. Courage will allow children to accept and face their difficulties so they can reach the career they desire.

Teaching Perseverance
Tips for Parents

To stick to a purpose or aim; never giving up on what one has set out to do. To try, try, try again.

What children need to know about perseverance:

Everybody at some point in their lives has to learn things which are difficult or overwhelming. As long as you are willing to keep trying, you can learn most anything. Immediate rewards rarely happen. We must be willing to work and wait for the results.

To help children develop perseverance:

1. Take time to talk to your children about the importance of continuing to try to learn things which are hard.

2. Share books and stories which emphasize the importance of perseverance.

   • *The Little Engine That Could*, by Watty Piper

   • *Amazing Grace*, by Mary Hoffman

   • *Try, Try Again*, and *Persevere*, in *The Children's Book of Virtues*, by William Bennett

3. Help your children set goals, and keep track of steps of progress toward those goals.

4. Share with your children the 3R's of perseverance:

   • **REMIND:** Remind yourself of the goal you want to achieve.

   • **REASSURE:** Reassure yourself that you can complete the task.

   • **RECOMMIT:** Recommit yourself to put forth your best effort into completing the goal.

The career connection:

Successful people are not necessarily the people who are the smartest. Successful people are those who keep trying and don't give up until they reach their goals. With perseverance people reach educational and career goals, and are able to have the career they desire.

Teaching Citizenship
Tips for Parents

Learning the importance of contributing to school and community. Having compassion and showing kindness through serving and helping others.

What children need to know about citizenship:

Our schools and communities are better places when everyone contributes by serving and helping one another.

1. Always model showing kindness and helping others.

2. Encourage your children to help you pick up trash in your neighborhood, donate non-perishable food to a food bank, and/or sponsor a child living in a poor country.

3. Encourage your children to join service organizations which focus on helping others.

4. Review the school's conflict management program with your children and provide praise when conflicts are handled well.

The career connection:

At work we must help each other accomplish our tasks. With teamwork, employees work more effectively together and much more gets accomplished. Businesses want to hire those who are loyal and are team players.

The Character & Career Connection published by National Center for Youth Issues, Chattanooga, TN.

75

Resources & References

Online Resources:

www.act.org/wwm/overview.html
World-Of-Work Map, Career Clusters
and Career Areas

www.armorepenguin.com/wordsearch

www.avatar-resources.com/honesty.cfm
Honesty in the workplace

www.bus.umich.edu/FacultyResearch/Research/CascadingEffects
Michigan Business School, "Cascading
Effects of Compassion Impact Employees
and Workplaces"

www.charactereducation.com/business.htm
The Character Development Group,
Dr. Phillip F. Vincent

www.ethics.org/character
The Ethics Resource Center,
Washington, DC

www.ethics.org/nbes2003
2003 National Business Ethics Survey

www.globalethics.org/corp/bizstats.html
The Institute for Global Ethics—
Business Statistics

www.inspirationalstories.com
After Hours Inspirational Stories

www.itstime.com
Respect in the Workplace—
Online Newsletter

www.quotegarden.com
The Quote Garden

Books

Bender, J. and A. Murray (2003). *Perfect Pals: How to Juggle Your Way From Perfection to Excellence*. Chattanooga, TN: National Center for Youth Issues.

Bennett, William J., 1995, *The Children's Book of Virtues*, "*Try, Try Again and Persevere*," New York, NY, Simon & Schuster Adult Publishing Group.

Carlson, Nancy, 1982, *Harriet and the Roller Coaster*, Minneapolis, MN, Carolrhoda Books, Inc.

Dr. Seuss, 1940, *Horton Hatches the Egg*, New York, NY, Random House.

Duran, Maureen (1995). *Kids With Character: Character Building Activities for the Elementary Classroom*. Chantilly, Virginia: A Choice in Education.

Hoffman, Mary, 1991, *Amazing Grace*, New York, NY, Penguin Putnam Inc.

Lickona, Thomas (1991). *Educating For Character: How Our Schools Can Teach Respect and Responsibility*. New York, NY: Bantam Books.

Long, Betty (1995). *Careers and Me*. Itasca, IL: The Riverside Publishing Co.

Pinkney, Jerry, 2000, *Aesop's Fables*, "*The Tortoise and the Hare*," New York, NY, Sea Star Books a division of North – South Books, Inc.

Piper, Watty, 1976, *The Little Engine That Could*, New York, NY, Platt and Munk Publishers.

Rich, Dorothy (1992). *MegaSkills: In School and in Life—The Best Gift You Can Give Your Child.* New York, NY: Houghton Mifflin.

Silverstein, Shel, 1964, *The Giving Tree,* New York, Evanston and London, Harper & Row Publishers.

Notes